Circe Invidiosa

Sonata No. 1 for the Piano

Tom Gerou

Edited by Albert Mendoza

Alfred Music
P.O. Box 10003
Van Nuys, CA 91410-0003
alfred.com

ISBN-10: 1-4706-1842-7
ISBN-13: 978-1-4706-1842-1

Cover art: *Circe Invidiosa*, 1892 (oil on canvas), by John William Waterhouse (1849–1917)

Poem: *Circe Invidiosa*, 2014, by Catherine Seitz Nichols
Used by Permission.

FOREWORD

ABOUT THE PAINTING

English painter John William Waterhouse (1849–1917) worked in *Pre-Raphaelite style*, an artistic movement popular in the mid to late 19th century that emphasized bold colors, fine details, and compositional complexity. Although known for this style, elements of the Impressionist movement also influenced Waterhouse's work, particularly the use of color to generate atmosphere and mood. His oil paintings predominately portray the myths and legends of ancient Greek mythology or English Arthurian tales. He frequently painted women, often on large canvases, capturing their beauty and innocence but also turning them, through careful attention to facial expression and posture, into emotionally distracted central figures. Waterhouse continued producing Pre-Raphaelite paintings long after the style had fallen out of vogue; however, more than a century later, several major art galleries display his work, allowing appreciative new audiences to find his expressive canvases.

In 1892, Waterhouse completed *Circe Invidiosa*, the second of three depictions of Circe, the mythological Greek goddess of magic and sorcery. (See front cover.) The other two Circe paintings by Waterhouse are *Circe Offering the Cup to Ulysses* (1891) and *The Sorceress* (ca. 1911). The episode portrayed in *Circe Invidiosa* captures the moment when Circe, tormented by envy for the attentions of the seagod Glaucus, poisons the water where her rival Scylla bathes. (*Invidiosa* is the Latin word for envious.) The tainted water transforms the beautiful Scylla into a hideous creature. The depiction of Circe as a youthful beauty, quietly controlled and focused, contrasts with the frenetic motion of her hair whirled by the rising vapors of the newly born monster below her feet. Waterhouse uses a vivid green in the stream of water flowing from the bowl-like cup in Circe's hands. It creates a lush foil to the deep blue gown of the powerful sorceress.

ABOUT THE MUSIC

Waterhouse's *Circe Invidiosa*, with its underlying structure but dramatic emotion, easily lends itself to musical reinterpretation.

Circe Invidiosa: Sonata No. 1 is a one-movement sonata written in sonata-allegro form, although it does not adhere to the tonic-dominant harmonic relationships found in traditional sonatas. Instead, the harmonic framework of the piece uses *mediant relationships*, ascending or descending progressions by 3rds, to support its contrasting themes. These types of harmonic relationships are abundant in the works of late Romantic and Impressionist composers, who were contemporaries of Waterhouse. An example of this harmonic movement by 3rds can be found in the opening of the sonata when, at measure 6, the A-flat major harmony (the tonic) shifts to an E dominant chord (a chord a 3rd below the tonic). In contrast to the use of mediant relationships, dominant harmonies only occasionally influence the large scale, structural harmonic progressions. Most notably, in measures 182–186, the dominant, in a *marcato* flourish, leads to the arrival of the A-flat major recapitulation at measure 187. Later, the subdominant becomes the climactic focus of the composition when it appears before the coda in alternation with the tonic (mm. 281–314), anchoring the entire piece with a powerful, *deciso* (resolute) sentiment.

Rhythm plays a central role in this sonata. The unstable pulse throughout the piece, created by constantly changing meters, produces a toccata-like effect reminiscent of the maniacal Circe depicted by Waterhouse—highly controlled yet driven by passion. Melodically, two themes are clearly presented in the sonata's exposition. The opening first theme is characterized by rapid, arpeggiated flourishes and a texture that requires the performer to play with interlocked hands. Two-hand arpeggios moving swiftly up the keyboard depict the swirling waters of Scylla's pool. The tender *Andante con moto* second theme, beginning at measure 50, is marked by increasingly sinister-sounding chromaticism. These two themes are manipulated in the development, which begins softly at measure 109. Throughout the piece, short motives combine with intricate rhythms and sonorities to convey the introspection, internal conflict, and passion within Waterhouse's *Circe Invidiosa*. This tension gradually unwinds as the piece nears its conclusion; however, the peaceful character lasts only momentarily. The coda (mm. 330–345), a sequence of descending gestures marked *cresc. e accel. poco a poco*, represents the pouring of potion from Circe's cup down to the *feroce* (ferocious) transformation at her feet.

– Tom Gerou

This work was jointly commissioned by Music Teachers National Association
and North Dakota Music Teachers Association in 2014

Circe Invidiosa
Sonata No. 1 for the Piano

Tom Gerou

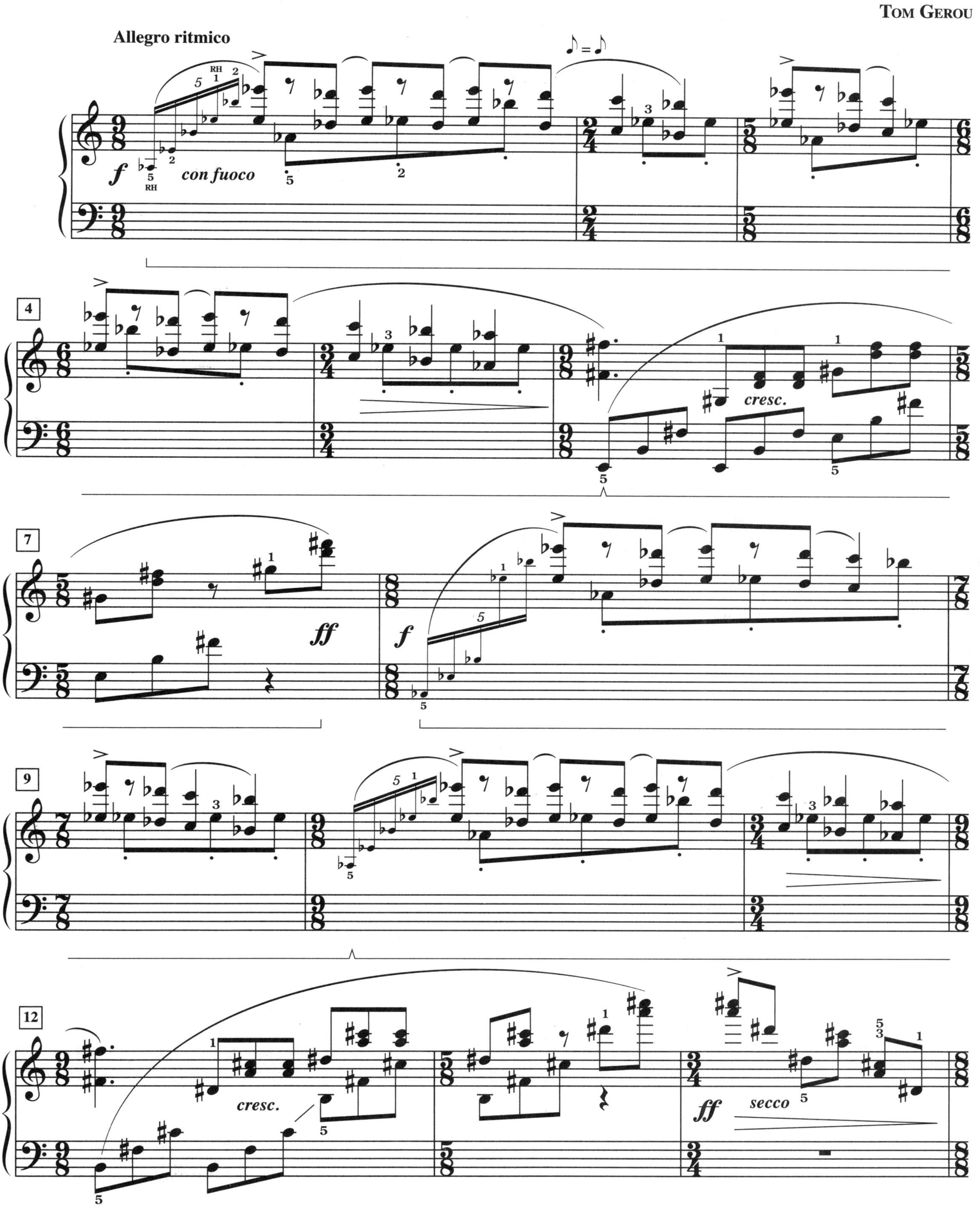

15
mf
giocoso
quasi pizzicato
19
f
cresc.
ff
22
mf
f
25
cresc.
29
ff
secco
f

32
35
38
41
45
cresc.
ff
8va
(sopra)
molto rit.
f
p

Andante con moto

agitato non troppo
71
p
76
mp
p
mp
81
mf
p
86
allargando
mf
90

93
più mosso
f
96
mf
mp
100
p
104
rit. e dim. poco a poco
perdendosi
Tempo I
109
pp
(sopra)

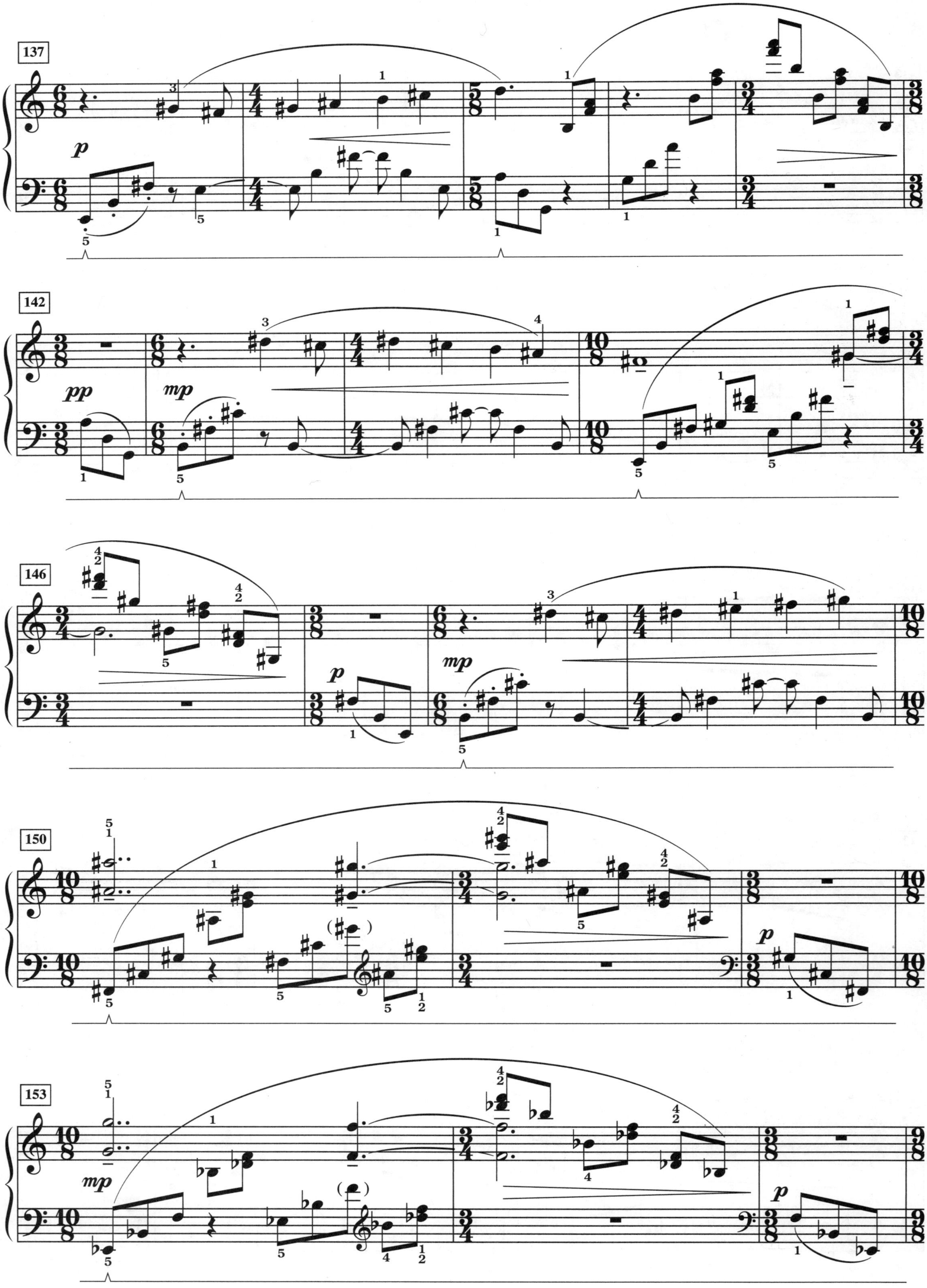
137
p
142
pp
mp
146
p
mp
150
p
153
mp
p

156
mp
8va
4
4
1
1
5
2
(sopra)
non rit.
2
2
p
5
1
162
mp
4
3
2
2
5
5
166
4
3
2
2
1
5
5
170
mf
4
3
2
5
1
5
174
Poco allargando
f
più f
molto cresc.
5
5
1
5

199
mf giocoso
quasi pizzicato
203
f
cresc.
207
ff   mf
f
211
cresc.
215
ff
f

218
221
224
227
231
cresc.
ff
f
8va
(sopra)
molto rit.
p

Andante con moto

275
più mosso
278
ff   deciso
282
286
290
f

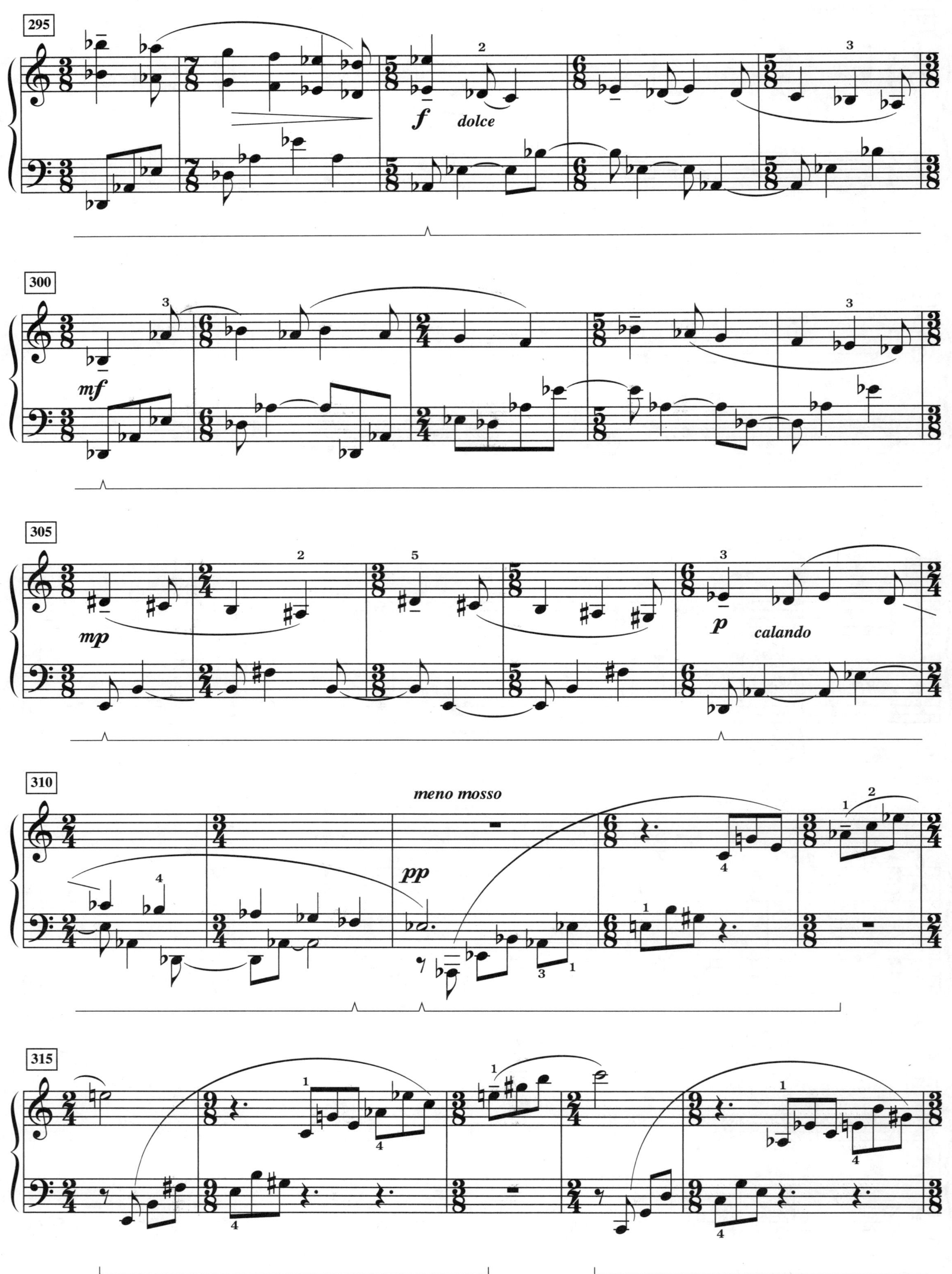
295
f dolce
300
mf
305
mp
p calando
310
meno mosso
pp
315

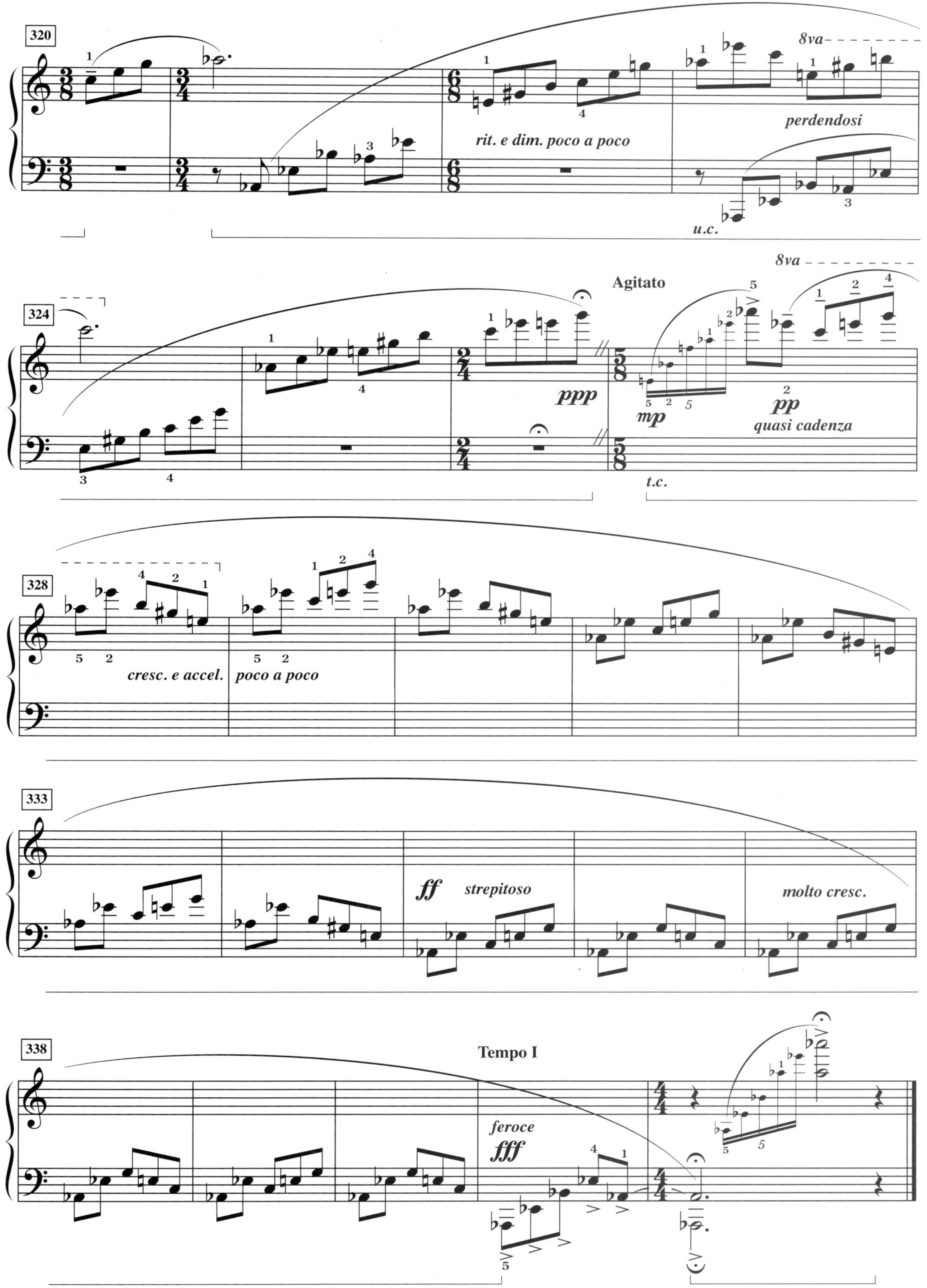
320
3/8 3/4 6/8
rit. e dim. poco a poco
8va
perdendosi
u.c.
324
Agitato
8va
ppp
mp
pp
quasi cadenza
t.c.
2/4 5/8
328
cresc. e accel. poco a poco
5 2 5 2
333
ff strepitoso
molto cresc.
338
Tempo I
feroce
fff
4/4
4/4

Circe Invidiosa

by Catherine Seitz Nichols
(2014)

Eyes flash like waves near crashing,
throwing thunderbolts of despair.
Glaucus swims to me, an eel flowing,
seal-slick tail and seagrass hair.

"Give me a cup of love," he pleads,
"to turn Scylla's gaze to me.
She is the one pearl my heart needs
 in this cold and lonely sea!"

Through froth-grey fog
I find her, nothing more
than a simple pebble washed upon
my mind's sharp and rocky shore.

Her pale eyes must be broken
to miss the breathless beauty in
each curve of every glistening scale—
a divine man wearing fish's skin.

How could she coldly refuse
to be his honored bride,
when his whole being is infused
by the power of surging tides?

I tell him I will help him,
and in that vow, I do not lie—
the dark magics I brew in my cup
offer gifts of deeper sight.

Smoldering branches, burn deceptions,
baneful leaves and flowers decay.
Fruit of truth—a revelation.
In this cup, the light of day.

Be revealed, scuttling cruelty.
Be revealed, heart's dismay.
Be revealed, false hounds of passion.
With this cup, my will make way.

Not jealousy, but love's sacrifice—
a heart cracked pure and cruel
tips the cup into the bath
and poisons Scylla's pool.

Truth strips the mask of comely skin,
lets loose the spectacle that lies within
the needle teeth, the shrieking bark—
an endless thrash of tentacled arms.

She will screech for all eternity
astride harrowing rocks displayed,
a warning to all unlucky sailors
who dare steer their ships this way.